The
COMPLEAT GOLFER

By the la' Harry
This shall not go for Nothing

COCK OF THE GREEN.

Portrait of the original golfing maniac, Andrew McKellar, died c. 1813. He played at Bruntsfield near Edinburgh and became so obsessed that he neglected his business, played by day, and after dark by the light of a lantern, and made his wife bring his meals out to the course

Knickerbocker suit from an advertisement for golfing attire, 1875-1900

The COMPLEAT GOLFER

An illustrated history of the Royal and Ancient Game

**Ian T. Henderson
& David I. Stirk**

**London
Victor Gollancz Ltd
1984**

Copyright © Henderson & Stirk Ltd
1982

First published October 1982 by
Victor Gollancz Ltd
14 Henrietta Street
London WC2E 8QJ

Second impression December 1982
Third impression April 1984

Created for the publishers by
Lund Humphries Publishers Ltd,
London

Designed by Christine Charlton
Typeset in Plantin by
TNR Productions Ltd, London
Printed in Great Britain by
Lund Humphries, Bradford

British Library Cataloguing in
Publication Data
Henderson, Ian T.
  The compleat golfer.
  1. Golf—History
  I. Title   II. Stirk, David I.
  796.352   GV963

  ISBN 0-575-03218-9

All the illustrations reproduced in this
book are taken from *Golf in the Making*
or *Royal Blackheath* published by
Henderson & Stirk Ltd

Contents

Introduction   page   7

The Origins of Golf   10

Dutch Golf   12

Early Golf   18

The Golf Ball   28

Early Clubmakers   41

Wooden Clubs   52

The Iron Clubmakers and Iron Clubs   60

Golfing Styles   70

Patents   74

Golfing Costume   78

Memorabilia   87

A sketch taken from Lauthier's *Treatise*
(Paris, 1717)) showing jeu de mail
(pall mall) being played (see page 11)

Introduction

This book presents the pictorial history of the 'Royal and Ancient' game of golf.

It is widely believed among golfers that the game originated in Scotland. In fact, as we now know, it was the Dutch who appear to have invented it, playing a game called *Spel meten Kolven* from 1296 until the beginning of the eighteenth century when, mysteriously, this early form of golf went out of fashion and another game called 'Het Kolven', a sort of mini-golf, often played indoors, took its place. Records exist of golf being played in forty Dutch townships, with edicts against playing the game in the streets. By the end of the sixteenth century, Dutch and Flemish artists were sketching and painting, in dozens of landscapes and on a wealth of tiles, a remarkable record of life in Holland; and there is abundant evidence from these illustrations that life in Holland at this period included the game of golf.

There were close ties between Scotland and Holland during the fifteenth and sixteenth centuries and golf first appeared in Scotland and the east coast ports which traded with Holland. It is significant that golf did not appear on the west coast of Scotland until much later. Whereas golf in Holland was a national game, it never became so in Scotland because of its considerable expense until the great golf craze arrived in the 1890s.

The establishment of golf in Britain can now definitely be attributed to groups of freemasons who formed the first Golfing Societies and played golf as a healthy form of exercise prior to wining and dining. Golf was not the prime reason for forming a Society at that time. The record of six early Golfing Societies (the Royal Burgess Golfing Society of Edinburgh, the Honourable Company of Edinburgh Golfers, the Royal and Ancient Golf Club of St Andrews, the Bruntsfield Golf Club, the Royal Musselburgh Golf Club and the Royal Blackheath Golf Club) reveal evidence of masonic rites, uniforms, bet books, and golf on a course of 5 holes followed by ceremonial dinners.

The great development of the game can be attributed to the wonderful strides made in perfecting the ball; and the arrival of the rubber golf ball in 1848 made the game considerably cheaper and therefore available to more people. Prior to that date, when the feathery ball was in use, golf clubs had long, wooden heads; a single iron club might be in the player's bag for use in really difficult situations but the main reason why iron clubs were not used more often was because the feathery ball could easily be burst by an iron club and at that time balls were as expensive as clubs. With the arrival of the rubber ball iron clubs were used increasingly and before long there were more iron clubs than wooden ones in the golf bag; and there were many more golfers. Nevertheless, golf did not become a national game in Scotland until the 1890s when it spread all over the world, particularly to the USA. To the Scots, therefore, must be given the credit for keeping the game alive for so many years and preserving it for posterity. It was they who were to make it so popular throughout the world, and thousands of Scotsmen left their shores to establish and teach the game in the farthest corners of the earth.

Those readers who wish to pursue the history of golf in greater detail are referred to two other books by the authors: Ian T. Henderson and David I. Stirk: *Golf in the Making* (1979) which contains all that is known about early club- and ball-makers, the club themselves, patents, etc.; and *Royal Blackheath* (1981) which explains how groups of Freemasons were responsible for the formation of the first Golfing Societies and how the Royal Blackheath Golf Club itself helped to spread the game throughout England and other parts of the world.

Match at Blackheath, by F. Gilbert,
1869

The Origins of Golf

That golf is an ancient game is undeniable but its origins and its relationship with other games which involved striking a ball with some form of club have so far not been resolved. The Romans played a game called 'Paganica' using a leather ball stuffed with flock and in England in the fourteenth century a similar game called 'cambuca' was played with a wooden ball, but we do not know what kind of club was used to hit the ball in either case.

The sketch of the stained-glass roundel from the Battle of Crecy window in Gloucester Cathedral, *c.* 1350, and the Araucanian Indian boy from Chile, taken from *The Zoology of the Voyage of HMS Beagle* which describes Charles Darwin's famous voyage *c.* 1835 are illustrations whose resemblance must be accepted as a coincidence. There is no clue as to what form of game is being played, and all that can be deduced is that from early times in various parts of the world striking a ball with a stick was a form of activity that attracted adherents — call it what you will

Pall mall, or jeu de mail, the stroke for which, from all descriptions, closely resembled the golf swing as shown on page 6. The game originated in Italy, was taken up by the French and came to England early in the seventeenth century. The original course in London was Pall Mall, St James's. This was later moved to The Mall, and both names recall their original use to this day. The pair of clubs and a wooden ball taken from a house at No. 68 Pall Mall still survive in the British Museum. It is hard to see how this game, from which croquet originated, could have influenced the development of golf

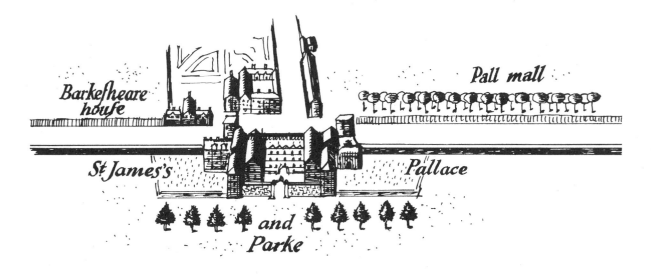

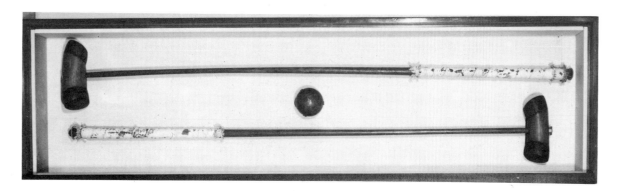

Dutch Golf

The beginnings of golf have been traced to the village of Loenen in 1296 and there are documentary records of the game being played in no less than forty places in Holland. There were frequent edicts banning play in the streets and city authorities were forever attempting to confine players to areas outside the city on the ramparts. In the winter the game was played on the ice.

Pictures from the sixteenth and seventeenth centuries provide an illustrated golfing record unique in the annals of any sport. The marvellous Dutch landscape paintings of these years show that people in Holland were playing a form of golf, with enthusiasm, up to the early eighteenth century, when the game inexplicably died out. In many a crowded scene, on ice or land, tiny figures may be observed, club in hand. There are numerous portraits of children holding a club rather than a toy, and, in all, there are nearly 500 illustrations, together with a fascinating number of Dutch tiles, all of which relate to the game.

So far no contemporary description of the game or its rules has been found but there is evidence of a hole being used, and on ice a pole, often decorated, was adopted instead.

We show on page 16 early seventeenth-century metal club heads and a wooden ball, with a modern ball for comparison, all found in excavations in Amsterdam. No example of a seventeenth-century wooden club has so far been found. Leather balls, stuffed with horsehair, flock or feathers were in general use and their mode of construction can be observed in many of the portraits. Similar types of balls were also produced in large numbers for hand tennis *(Kaatsen)*, an ancient game which is still played today. The ball manufacturers did a large export business throughout the Continent and also shipped balls to Scotland (and there is evidence that Scotland, in turn, shipped wooden clubs to Holland in the mid-seventeenth century). The ball-making craft survives to this day.

When the game died out and all evidence of play disappeared, its place was taken by *Kolf,* or *Het Kolven,* a short distance (and often indoor) game, which might be termed mini-golf, using heavier rigid clubs and large balls. This game in turn was to lose its popularity, although still played when the Scottish version of the game arrived at The Hague in 1890.

One of the two maps on page 17 indicates the places where golf is known to have been played prior to 1700. It is clear from this and from contemporary pictures that the Dutch game of golf was a national game. The other map shows the places in Scotland were golf is believed to have been played, circa 1650. These coastal regions were places where trade with Holland was likely to have been carried on. It is not without significance that golf did not spread to the west of Scotland until the middle of the nineteenth century. Whereas golf in Holland was a national game, it never became really popular in Scotland on account of the considerable expense of playing, until the great golf craze at the end of the nineteenth century.

A player with the ball teed up in the snow

Sketch after a Flemish Book of Hours, 1501

Sketches of golfers extracted from
seventeenth-century Dutch landscapes

Early seventeenth-century club
fragments and wooden ball with
modern ball for comparison

Wooden ball, *c.* 1590

Leather-covered ball enlarged from
sketch below (*c.* 1612)

Taken from a painting by an unknown
Flemish artist, and reputed to be the
eldest son of James I in 1595

Golf in progress, supported by the
necessary refreshment. After Hendrick
Avercamp

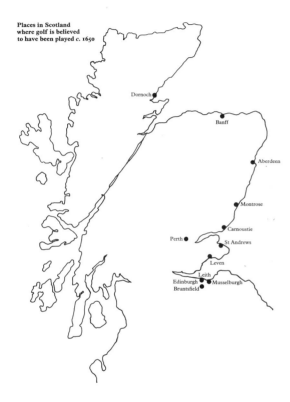

Places in Scotland
where golf is believed
to have been played c. 1650

Dornoch

Banff

Aberdeen

Montrose

Carnoustie

Perth

St Andrews

Leven

Leith
Edinburgh   Musselburgh
Bruntsfield

Places in Scotland where golf is
believed to have been played c. 1650

Places in The Netherlands
where golf was played prior
to 1700

● before 1400
■ before 1500
○ before 1600
□ before 1700

○8   12□   13□

14□

○3   17□

6□
19□ 5■

□15   1●   □16

□18

□11
○10   7■

2●

●4

○9

1	Loenen aan de Vecht	1297	11	The Hague	1609
2	Brielle	1387	12	Hoorn	c 1610
3	Haarlem	1390	13	Enkhuizen	1612
4	Dordrecht	1401	14	Kampen	c 1615
5	Naarden	1456	15	Leyden	1637
6	Amsterdam	1480	16	Utrecht	1637
7	Arnhem	c 1490	17	Zwolle	c 1640
8	Alkmaar	c 1550	18	Doesburg	c 1640
9	Antwerp	1553	19	Ouderkerk	1659
10	Delft	1587			

Prepared by S. van Hengel

Places in the Netherlands where golf
was played prior to 1700

Early Golf

Bruntsfield, Edinburgh, with a view of the Castle in the background and the Golfers' Inn, which still stands today, in the foreground. A watercolour painted by Paul Sandby RA in 1746 (courtesy of the Trustees of the British Museum). The site of the course still exists but the view of the Castle is obstructed. Visitors may still pitch and putt there with replicas of the old long-headed wooden clubs

William St Clair of Roslin. Grand Master Mason of Scotland: he laid the foundation stone of the Golf House at Leith in 1767 for the Company of Edinburgh Golfers, assisted by fourteen 'worthy members of the golfing company', all Masons

Above left: Portrait of Old Alick, the hole-maker at Royal Blackheath

Left: the oldest surviving hole-cutter, dated 1829, Royal Musselburgh

Above: 'Stymied', from a Dublin print

Before the days of a regulation hole and teeing ground, the ball was teed up with sand taken from the bottom of the hole, either one or two club-lengths from it. This photograph was taken at Edinburgh, c. 1860

Left: Edward, Prince of Wales at Oxford in 1912, about to bicycle off to play golf

Mr. William Thomson   Admiral Maitland Dougall   Sandy Pirie   Colonel Jo, Fairlie   Tom Morris
   Mr. George Whyte Melville   Mr. George Glennie   Mr. Gilmour
PLAYERS AT ST. ANDREWS IN THE 'SIXTIES'

The picture above shows a group of professionals at St Andrews in the 1860s

A *Punch* cartoon of the 1890s with the caption 'The Golf Stream' — a comment on the golf craze of the time

'Holed Out' — Louis Wain, the Victorian artist who drew cats as humans, catches the spirit of the age

The first golfing society in England was established on the Heath at Blackheath, London. Above: The Green Man public house, for many years the headquarters of the Royal Blackheath Club, now demolished

Medal day at Royal Blackheath, 1875

The Gold Medal shown here is the oldest in the history of the game and dates from 1792 when it was made for the Knuckle Club, a Masonic organisation subsequently disbanded, 'the members in future merely to meet as golfers'

Another example of an early gold medal from Loretto House Golf Club, Musselburgh, 1854

Professionals playing at Royal
Blackheath, 1890

Sketch taken from the centre design of
the Knuckle Club Medal

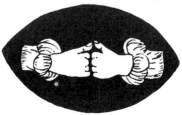

Some cartoons which appeared in
Punch around the turn of the century

THE AMERICAN HUSBAND

THE ENGLISH WIFE

In America the ladies, from the beginning, refused to accept a subordinate position in golf, unlike their British counterparts who, whether they liked it or not, were not welcomed as club members. Even today this situation exists in a few clubs

LINK(S)ED SWEETNESS

The Real Caddie (audibly). " This club is going to ruin—
allowing all these ladies to join ! "
Miss Sharp. " They evidently can't get gentlemen ! "

The first Ladies' Golf Club at
Westward Ho!, was formed in 1868.
The Ladies had their own 9-hole
course, separate from the main course,
and their own professional, who was
only allowed to teach them. All is
decorum in this picture; it is clearly
more important not to show an ankle
than to have a good golf swing; nor did
the decorative dress suggest that a full
golf swing was possible. The clubhouse
is a tent, erected for the day

26

Willie Dunn Jr. (1865-1952) was
Professional Champion of America,
1894. He designed and constructed the
course at Shinnecock Bay, Long
Island, USA, c. 1890

Charles B. Macdonald, the first official
winner of the American amateur title,
in 1895. His family originally came
from St Andrews. He subsequently
took a leading part in promoting the
game, in forming the U.S. Golf
Association and in maintaining its
links with St Andrews, thus ensuring
that the world still plays under the
same rules

The Golf Ball

The great development of the game of golf can be directly attributed to progress made in perfecting the ball, making it a more pleasant game to play. The ball in use until the middle of the nineteenth century was what is known as a 'feathery'. This was a leather ball — not unlike a fives ball to look at — stuffed with wet feathers, which became very hard when it dried out. It flew when dry, but wheezed through the air in wet conditions and could easily be destroyed by an injudicious stroke with an iron club. At a price of up to 4s 0d each, the feathery ball was expensive, costing almost as much as a club. The most important development in the history of golf was the use of rubber in making a ball. 'Gutta percha', a hard substance which could be softened in hot water, was discovered in Malaya in 1843. In 1848 the first rubber golf-balls appeared, made very simply by immersing the 'gutta percha' in hot water and rolling it by hand into round balls, which hardened as they dried out. These smooth round balls, however, would not fly properly at first, but it was discovered that this defect could be rectified by indenting them with a hammer. They would not accept white paint and were dark yellow or brown in colour, but they were cheap and would last forever. This discovery immediately put the game within reach of those who could not afford the 'feathery'. By the 1880s the 'gutty' or hard composite ball began to appear —a ball so hard that it had a decisive effect on the design of wooden clubs. Club heads could shatter on impact. Sometimes even the balls themselves shattered.

Then out of the blue came the next great advance — the arrival in 1898 of the Haskell core-wound rubber ball, invented and developed in America. This at once made the game easier and more pleasant to play. The ball could fly yards further and even when mis-hit, the results were not so disastrous. This ball was relatively expensive, and cost 2s 6d, whereas iron clubs were 3s 6d and woods 5s 0d. But the improvement was so decisive that price did not matter. The innovation also affected every golf course, all of them in the end having to be lengthened to accommodate the new ball. It was not until 1922 that the size of the ball was first standardised (there are now two sizes). Before that any size of ball could be used. Today's ball is little recognised for the marvel of ingenuity that it is. A direct descendant of the Haskell, it is now at a price which, amazingly, is only a fraction of the price of a new club.

Golf balls prior to 1900

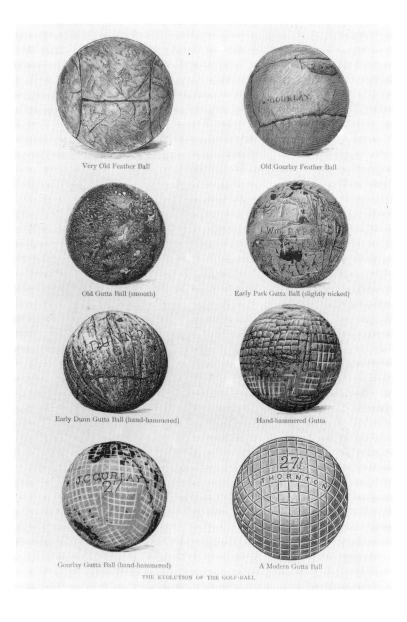

Very Old Feather Ball

Old Gourlay Feather Ball

Old Gutta Ball (smooth)

Early Park Gutta Ball (slightly nicked)

Early Dunn Gutta Ball (hand-hammered)

Hand-hammered Gutta

Gourlay Gutta Ball (hand-hammered)

A Modern Gutta Ball

THE EVOLUTION OF THE GOLF-BALL

Top (left to right): Dunlop Maxfli,
c. 1922; Rubber-cored Springvale
Hawk, c. 1907; Cestrian gutty, c. 1900.
Above: home-made gutta, and sheet of
gutta percha from which it was made

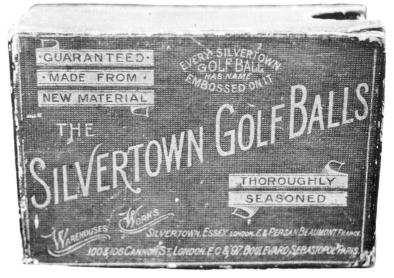

Golf-ball box

THE "ECLIPSE" GOLF BALL.
(CURRIE'S PATENT.)

THESE have quite superseded the old gutta-percha balls. They are almost indestructible, no club or iron will hack them, they fly beautifully, and retain their perfectly round shape; they can be driven further than the gutta-percha ball, and are quite true on the putting-green.

EXTRACT FROM "THE FIELD," 23RD JULY, 1881. —"We have thoroughly tested the specimens sent, and were agreeably surprised to find how near they came to the high estimate put upon them by the Patentee. Most assuredly they do not get hacked; not only did we play for four hours with the one ball, but for nearly two minutes afterwards we hammered away at it with our niblick, and no trace of hacking could be found. A better driving ball, too, we never struck; but the very elasticity which constituted its excellence in that particular at first rendered it somewhat uncertain in the short or putting game, especially where the green was a bit rough. That drawback, on our calling attention to it, the Patentee has remedied, and a fresh trial has convinced us that the remedy is effectual. As to the alterations effected by change of temperature, we cannot, in this tropical weather, speak from experience; but every Golfer knows that during intense frost the gutta-percha balls occasionally split, and these we are assured will not."

THE "ECLIPSE" GOLF BALL.—The "Eclipse" continues to grow in favour with golfers, as the unsolicited testimony of experts abundantly testifies. At the commencement of last season it for a time lost its good name; complaints as to chipping, splitting, and durability —or, rather, non-durability—were frequent, and, as the patentee speedily discovered, not without cause. The increased demand for the ball had necessitated the construction of new machinery, and in the augmented plant was found a flaw which accounted for the shortcoming. This, however, has since been remedied. A correspondent writes that he has played every alternate day for two months with a couple of these balls selected at random, and never drove any that gave such entire satisfaction.—*Field*, April 2nd, 1887.

Messrs. Currie, of the Caledonian Rubber Works, Edinburgh, are the patentees of the "Eclipse" Golf Ball, which, since they first introduced it, has been greatly improved in flying qualities. No less authority than Mr. Horace Hutchinson, the amateur champion, has pronounced the opinion that in its all round merit, the "Eclipse" is quite as good as the Gutta Ball. There can be no doubt about the "Eclipse" being the better ball to play with against the wind; it also retains its roundness, a great desideratum in putting, and is the most economical ball of the two.—The *Newcastle Daily Journal*, April 14th, 1887.

To be had from all Indiarubber Depots and Golf Club Makers.

PATENTEES AND SOLE MAKERS,
WILLIAM CURRIE & CO.,
Caledonian Rubber Works, Dalry Road, Edinburgh.

THE PLAIN SOLID
GUTTA PERCHA
BALL WITH
SCRATCHED OR
HAMMERED SUR-
FACE. THIS DIS-
PLACED THE
FEATHER BALL.

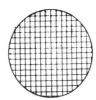

THE GUTTA
PERCHA BALL,
WITH CUT LINE
MARKING;
POPULAR FOR
A PERIOD.

THE GUTTA PERCHA
BALL WITH
BRAMBLE MARKING.
THIS WAS THE LAST
OF THE HOMO-
GENEOUS BALLS.

THE FIRST RUBBER-
CORED BALL (THE
"HASKELL") WITH
CORE OF RUBBER
THREAD WOUND
UNDER TENSION
AND COVER OF
GUTTA PERCHA.
FIRST USED IN
BRITAIN IN 1902.

BRITISH IMPROVE-
MENT ON THE
HASKELL, WITH
LARGER CORE
AND SOLID
CENTRE.

FURTHER IMPROVE-
MENT; CORE AGAIN
LARGER AND
THE COVER MUCH
THINNER.

STILL LARGER
CORE AND "EGG-
SHELL" COVER.

A NEW DEPARTURE.
DIAMETER OF BALL
REDUCED FROM
$1\frac{11}{16}$ INCH TO $1\frac{5}{8}$,
WEIGHT IN PROPOR-
TION.

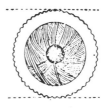

BALL OF NORMAL
SIZE BUT MUCH
HEAVIER THAN
BEFORE. FIRST
BALL TO SINK
IN WATER.

THE 1911 BALL.
SMALL SIZE ($1\frac{5}{8}''$)
AGAIN AND MUCH
HEAVIER THAN
BEFORE; SINKS IN
WATER.

Sketches of new developments for
balls and cover markings, taken from
Frys magazine 1911-12

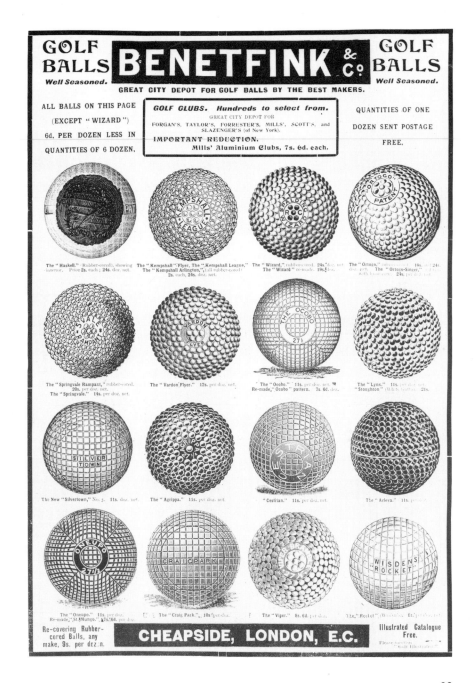

33

34

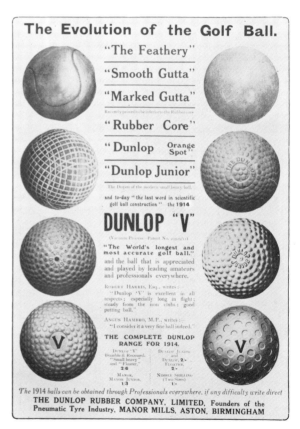

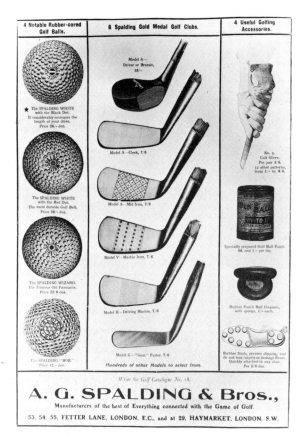

Early Clubmakers

Prior to the great golf craze which started in the last quarter of the nineteenth-century, the craft of making golf clubs and balls had been for many years confined to a few golfing families in Scotland where the art had been passed from father to son. These families were the Forgans, to whom the renowned H. Philp was related, the McEwans, the Dunns, the Patricks and the Parks. Here are staff photographs of R. Forgan & Son taken in 1881 and 1895

The McEwans

This club-making business was founded by James McEwan at Bruntsfield, Edinburgh, in 1770 and was carried on by three succeeding generations of the family until 1897

In 1847 they opened a branch at Musselburgh where at a later stage they also became ball-makers. This business was wound up in 1897

A group of old time professionals, Perth, 1864, including (1) Tom Morris, Jr. (2) Tom Morris, Sr. (3) G. D. Brown (4) D. Park (5) W. Dow (6) C. Hunter (7) W. Park (8) James Johnstone (9) J. Strath (10) R. Macdonald (11) R. Andrews

Peter McEwan 1834-1895

D. McEwan 1869-1921

Peter McEwan 1781-1836

MR. McEWAN'S PREMISES AT BRUNTSFIELD LINKS, EDINBURGH.

Willie Dunn Sr., 1821-1871

Jamie Dunn 1821-1878

The Dunns
The Dunn Family story starts with the twin brothers Willie and Jamie of Musselburgh, the sons of a plasterer. Together they achieved fame as golfers in a number of celebrated challenge matches for wagers. In 1851 Willie was appointed 'Keeper of the Green' at Blackheath where he stayed for fourteen years and was joined by his brother Jamie in 1854

Willie had two sons Tom (1849-1902) and Willie Jr. (1865-1952). Tom became one of the early golf-course architects and laid out some 137 courses. Willie Jr. went to America, laid out the famous course at Shinnecock Bay, Long Island, and in 1894 won the first unofficial championship of the USA. He was also in demand as a golf-course architect

Willie Dunn, Jr., Champion of
America 1894

Tom Dunn 1849-1902

45

Old Willie won the championship in 1860, 1863, 1866 and 1875 and, having been apprenticed as a ball-maker, set up as a club- and ball-maker in 1870 at Musselburgh. His brother Mungo won the championship in 1874, and his eldest son Willie Jr. in 1887 and 1889 as well as taking part in many challenge matches. He published the first book by a professional golfer on how to play the game of golf in 1896 and *The Art of Putting*, probably one of the only books on that subject, in 1920

Willie Park Sr., 1834-1903

Willie Park Jr., 1864-1925 Champion Golfer 1887

The Park family made an outstanding
contribution to golf in the hectic boom
years at the beginning of this century.
Willie Park Jr. was a dominant figure
of those days, top class golfer, leading
golf-course architect and maker of
clubs

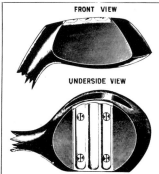

The Morris Family

Old Tom Morris was the son of a
hand-loom weaver and is without
doubt the greatest of all St Andrews'
historical figures. He won the
Championship Belt (precursor of the
Open Championship) in 1861, 1862,
1864 and 1867 and his son Tom
Morris Jr. won it outright by winning
three times in succession 1868-1869-
1870. Young Tom also won the first
Open Championship in 1872 but died
in 1875 following the tragic death of
his young wife, much lamented as the
finest golfer in his day

Old Tom became 'Keeper of the
Green' at St Andrews in 1864 and in
1867 he set up his own club-making
business which still survives today on
its original site

'Young Tom' and 'Old Tom' Morris,
c. 1873

Old Tom in later life

The Army & Navy Stores Catalogue *c.* 1900. Note that the public was still offered 'track-iron' style niblicks

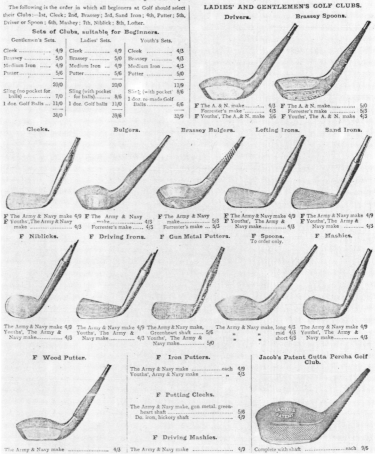

Ben Sayers in a bunker 1895 (The Redan Bunker, North Berwick)

Advertisement for Mills Aluminium clubs made by the Standard Golf Co., Sunderland. They produced clubs, mainly putters, from 1896 to the mid 1930s

'Wee' Ben Sayers and his son. Sayers (1857-1924) was a small man who originally trained as a circus acrobat; he often did cartwheels on the green when he holed a good putt

Slazenger and Sons catalogue — 1904

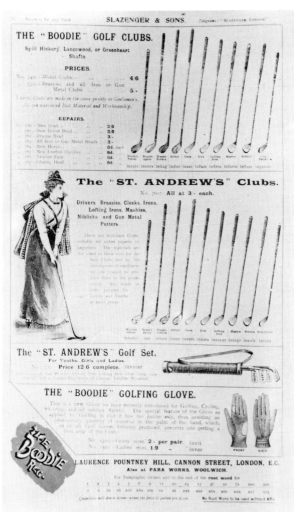

Wooden Clubs

Traditionally, the Keeper of the Green included in his duties the making and repairing of wooden clubs. He might be assisted by apprentices. The clubs were made or repaired by hand, and it was not until 1890-1900 that certain mechanical methods came to be employed. Clubs had individual characteristics, and owners, for this reason, preferred wherever possible to have them repaired rather than replaced. The relationship between the three parts of the club – grip, shaft and head – was complex and gave each club a unique feel which would have enabled its owner, even blindfolded, to identify it

The 'ancient' clubs of Royal Troon Golf Club. Features are the 'cut-off toe' shape of the irons; the shallow-faced, flat-lie woods. Several clubs have no grip

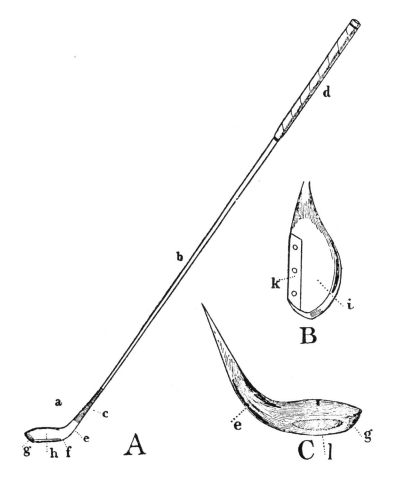

FIG. 1.—A WOODEN CLUB

A, the whole club; *B*, the 'sole'; *C*, back view of the head; *a*, the head; *b*, the shaft; *c*, the 'scare,' or part where head and shaft are fastened and bound together; *d*, the leather grip or handle; *e*, the neck; *f*, the heel; *g*, the toe or nose; *h*, the face; *i*, the sole; *k*, the bone; *l*, the lead.

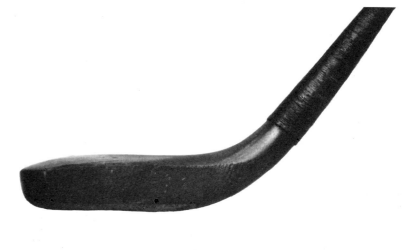

Two 'long-nosed' wooden club-heads made in the nineteenth-century. The shape of the head of the right-hand club is typical of the first part of the century, and that of the left-hand club of the second part

A driver by Hugh Philip of St Andrews

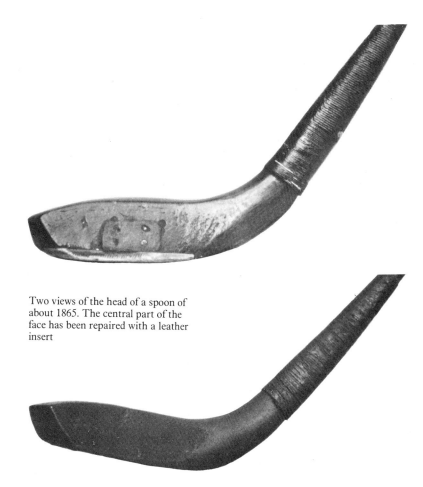

Two views of the head of a spoon of about 1865. The central part of the face has been repaired with a leather insert

The head of a baffing spoon. This club, shallow-faced and well-lofted, was used for approach shots before the days of iron play

A brassie by Harry Vardon, probably
1900. The small head is typical of this
era, as is the exceptionally long, fine
splice or scare. This club has a brass
sole, hence its name. Beneath the brass
is a horn insert in the leading edge.
Forerunner of the number 2 wood

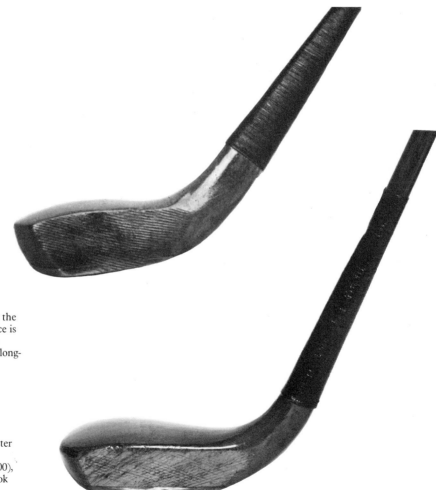

Two views of a 'bulger' driver.
Compared with long-nosed clubs, the
head is shorter and wider. The face is
deeper and is convex, rather than
concave. Such clubs replaced the long-
nosed clubs in about 1885

Hugh Philp (1782-1856) was Master
Club-maker of St Andrews. His
nephew, Robert Forgan (1824-1900),
joined him in the business and took
over when Philp died

The great amateur, George Glennie,
putting at Blackheath with a putting
cleek, c. 1885. It will be seen that the
green is merely an extension of the
fairway. There is no bag for carrying
clubs. The players all wear jackets

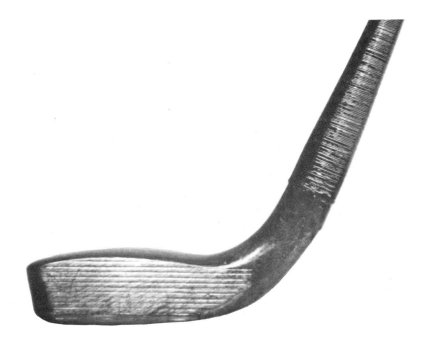

A wooden putter, made by William Park Jr., c. 1885

A scared-head club; somewhat more upright in lie than the other woods and with little loft. The shaft would be bowed, i.e. curved in the axis of toe to heel

The Iron Clubmakers
and Iron Clubs

J^N GRAY

Line drawings of cleek marks of various cleek-makers, the general term for iron club-makers. The heads of iron clubs were made by them, but the club was shafted and completed by the club-maker, who frequently had his name stamped on the back of the iron head

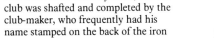 

Photos of cleek marks on clubs

In this picture, above the pipe of Stewart, the cleek-maker, is stamped the name of the man who shafted it, completed it and sold it

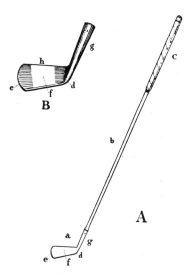

A. Wooden shafted iron club
B. Iron head with smooth face

A Philp/Forgan putter. This club has, in addition to a scared or scarffed joint, a long, narrow tongue-like mortice joint

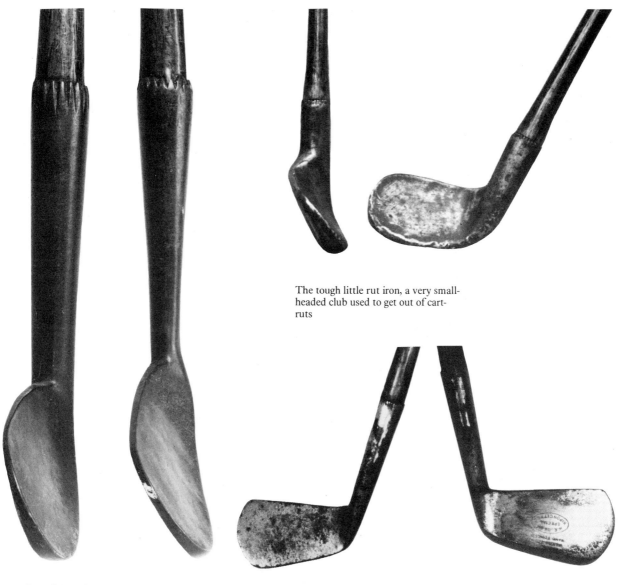

The tough little rut iron, a very small-headed club used to get out of cart-ruts

Iron clubs before 1830. The heads were blacksmith-made and the hammer marks can be seen in the faces, which are 'dished'

A 'tinned' mashie — a method of preventing rust

Two views of a lofting iron; precursor of the mashie, which in turn became a modern number 5 iron. 1875

Two views of a cleek, the earliest straight-faced iron. With modifications it became the modern number 1 and number 2 irons

Two views of a 'Maxwell' cleek. Holes were drilled in the hosel to lighten it

Two views of the mashie which first appeared in 1881 as a successor to the lofting iron

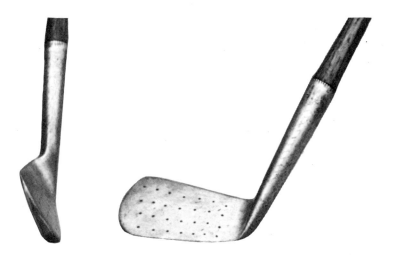

Two views of the 'Fairlie' niblick. This club had a hose, but no socket, thus eliminating 'shanking'

A putting cleek — a long, shallow face, like a cleek; it has less loft than a cleek, but more loft than a wooden putter. Useful, because of its loft, on rough greens

A wry-necked putter made by William Park, c. 1910. Park invented this shape of putter which is still in use today. It has less loft than the putting cleek

A 'water mashie'. The slots in the face allowed water (or sand) to pass through it

A selection of irons on the water mashie principle, offered for sale in a catalogue. The four clubs at the bottom, left and right, were known as 'rake' niblicks

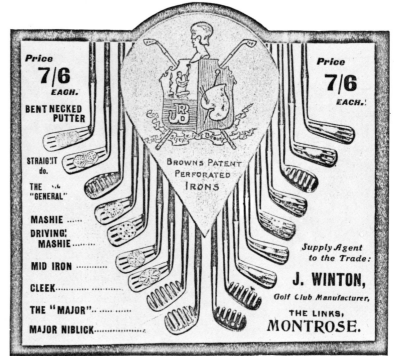

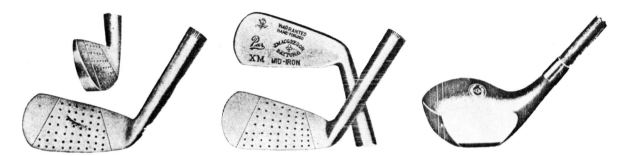

Guaranteed hand-forged par irons
from the catalogue of Crawford,
McGregor, Canby and Co. of the
USA. This firm was one of the first
American manufacturers of golf clubs,
starting in 1896

Golfing Styles

Tom Morris, showing the swing used for a feathery ball. Half way on the down swing. Note the flat plane in which the clubhead is swinging and the distance the ball is from the player. The stance is nearly square (but the ball being hit is a gutty, on this occasion)

The old palm grip. The club is held in the palm of the hands and not in the fingers. Common up to 1875

Two examples of the old St Andrews swing. Both elbows bent, the club dropped well down behind the back and almost touching the neck

Further golf swings. 2 and 3, the old St Andrews swing, showing the huge body turn. 1, 4, 5, 6 show less turn, the club near the horizontal and well clear of the neck: changes brought about by the improvement in golf balls towards the end of the nineteenth century

1

2

3

4

5

6

Various styles of putting

Harry Vardon and two aspects of his swing. Note the bent left arm. 6, on the previous page, is an earlier picture of him

Patents

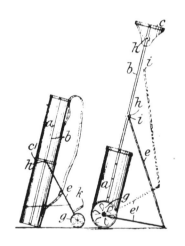

The golf trolley was first patented by Mr Boehmer in 1897. *Punch* produced an 'improved' version

MR. PUNCH'S PATENT CADDIE CAR

Before 1890 there were only fourteen patents which had anything to do with golf. Thereafter there was a flood of ideas which the Americans added to within ten years, most of them aimed at making the game easier to play. At that time there were no regulations as to the size or weight of golf balls and no regulations whatever relating to clubs until 1908; golf balls came under control in 1922. Many ideas appear today which were first thought of at the turn of the century.

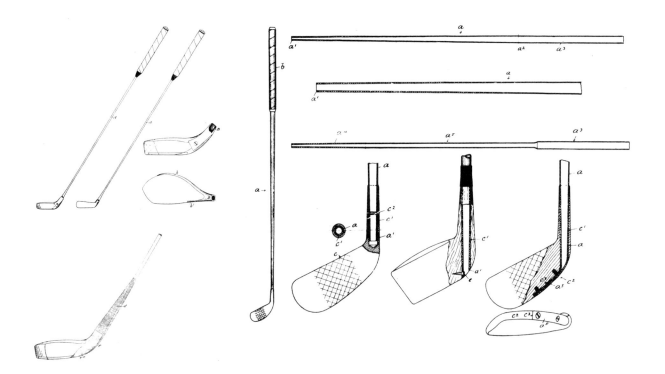

Steel Shafts

Mr T. A. Horsburgh of the Baberton
Club near Edinburgh in 1894 patented
and produced clubs with solid steel rod
shafts which were successfully used.
They failed to replace hickory-shafted
clubs because at that time the
professionals regarded them as a threat
to their livelihood

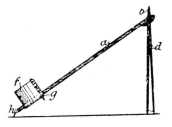

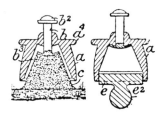

Above (top): a device for holding clubs and a tripod support, patented 1889; (centre) a device for moulding sand tees, and a rubber tee, both patented 1889; (bottom) mould for tees, patented 1885.
Below: ball pick-up, patented 1890

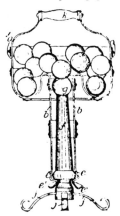

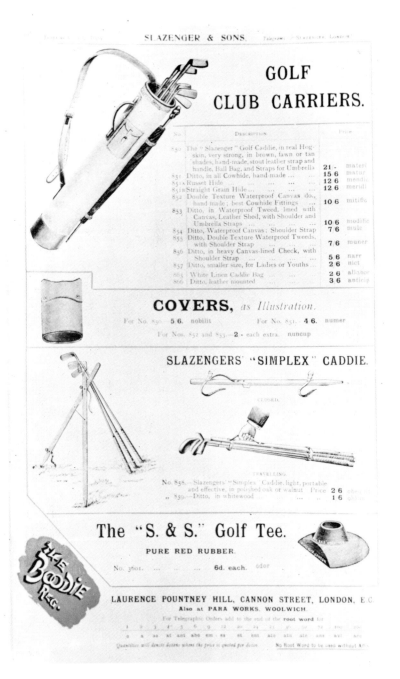

GOLF CLUB CARRIERS.

No.	Description	Price	
850	The "Slazenger" Golf Caddie, in real Hogskin, very strong, in brown, fawn or tan shades, hand-made, stout leather strap and handle, Ball Bag, and Straps for Umbrella	21 -	materi
851	Ditto, in all Cowhide, hand-made	15 6	matur
851A	Russet Hide	12 6	mendi
851B	Straight Grain Hide	12 6	meridi
852	Double Texture Waterproof Canvas do., hand-made; best Cowhide Fittings	10 6	mitific
853	Ditto, in Waterproof Tweed, lined with Canvas, Leather Shod, with Shoulder and Umbrella Straps	10 6	modific
854	Ditto, Waterproof Canvas; Shoulder Strap	7 6	mule
855	Ditto, Double Texture Waterproof Tweeds, with Shoulder Strap	7 6	muner
856	Ditto, in heavy Canvas-lined Check, with Shoulder Strap	5 6	narr
857	Ditto, smaller size, for Ladies or Youths	2 6	nict
865	White Linen Caddie Bag	2 6	allabor
866	Ditto, leather mounted	3 6	anticip

COVERS, *as Illustration.*

For No. 850. **5 6.** nobilit   For No. 851. **4 6.** numer

For Nos. 852 and 853. **2 -** each extra. nuncup

SLAZENGERS' "SIMPLEX" CADDIE.

No. 858.—Slazengers' "Simplex" Caddie, light, portable and effective, in polished oak or walnut Price 2 6   oberr
   859.—Ditto, in whitewood   1 6   oblitu

The "S. & S." Golf Tee.

PURE RED RUBBER.

No. 3601 ... ... 6d. each. odor

THE BOODIE BAG.

LAURENCE POUNTNEY HILL, CANNON STREET, LONDON, E.C.
Also at PARA WORKS, WOOLWICH.

For Telegraphic Orders add to the end of the **root word** for

Quantities will denote dozens where the price is quoted per dozen.   No Root Word to be used without Affix.

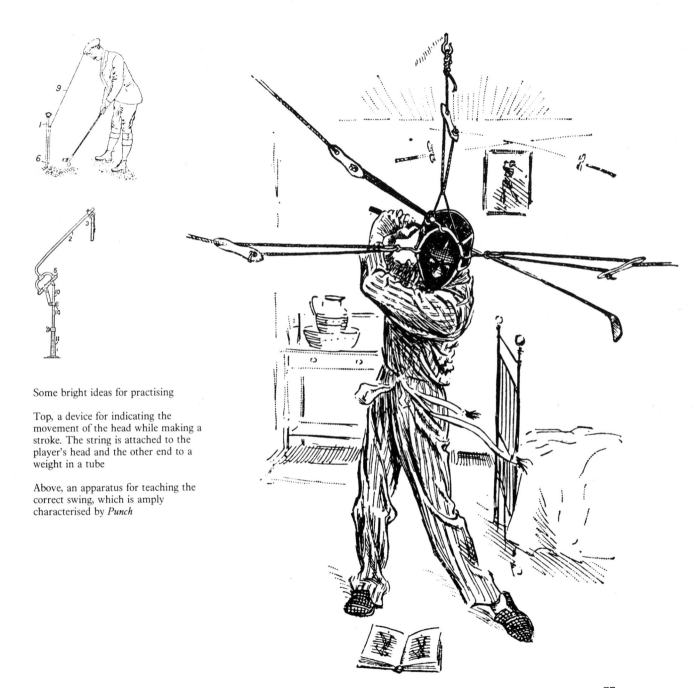

Some bright ideas for practising

Top, a device for indicating the movement of the head while making a stroke. The string is attached to the player's head and the other end to a weight in a tube

Above, an apparatus for teaching the correct swing, which is amply characterised by *Punch*

Golfing Costume

English golfing dress about 1875
There are no golf bags. The players
wear jackets and knickerbockers.
There are 'Tam O'Shanters' on some
heads — they were considered to lend
a Gaelic touch to the proceedings. The
caddies are barefoot, in contrast to the
slightly superior child in the lower
picture.

Advertisement for golfing attire 1875-1900

1 Jacket, tweed trousers and a bowler hat

2 The tweed knickerbocker suit

3 Similar; the caddie appears in some danger in this shot!

4 Knickerbocker suit

5 The 'Norfolk' jacket. Designed originally for shooting, it gave free shoulder movement

Advertisement for Ladies' golfing dress, 1875. Dress de rigueur — golf unlikely!

On windy days the long skirt could make it difficult to see the ball, so an elastic garter was worn at the waist, to be slipped down to about knee level to stop the skirt from billowing in the wind

1911. The lady manages very well despite the hat. She is showing an ankle!

1913. Miss Cecil Leitch wears a shorter skirt and spats over her shoes, and plays in a shirt and tie

W.J. Travis of the USA, winner of the British Amateur Championships, practising putting in 1904 with his centre-shafted 'Schenectady' putter. This type of putter was subsequently banned and remained so for many years except in the USA

1

2

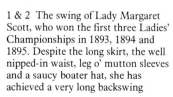
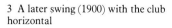

3

4

A view of Lady Margaret Scott, showing a small bustle to add to her problems

1 & 2 The swing of Lady Margaret Scott, who won the first three Ladies' Championships in 1893, 1894 and 1895. Despite the long skirt, the well nipped-in waist, leg o' mutton sleeves and a saucy boater hat, she has achieved a very long backswing

3 A later swing (1900) with the club horizontal

A Grand Match at St Andrews, 1850.
Painted by Charles Lees, R.A. The
players are dressed in swallow-tail
coats and three of them wear top hats
— the usual 'everyday' dress of the
landed gentry. There are no golf bags,
the clubs being carried under the arm

The Artisans' Golf Club, Northam,
Devon, 1888. They wear the working
man's 'everyday' dress; cloth caps,
jackets and serge trousers. No ties.
Boots with hob nails ('Tackety Boots')
much in evidence. They had no golf
bags because they could not afford
them, and only had a few clubs

A typical young caddie of about 1875.
He has no shoes or socks and his
trousers are probably 'cut-down cast-
offs' from his master. There were no
golf bags, so clubs were carried on the
shoulder or under the arm. Most of the
clubs are woods

Memorabilia

31.—THE DUFFER.

37.—A LONG PUTT.

16.—AN ANXIOUS
MOMENT.
"This for a Half."

2.—TOM MORRIS.
The G.O.M. of Golf.

29.—THE "MASHIE."

32.—LADY MARGARET
SCOTT.
Lady Champion 1893-4-5.

Part of a set of Cope Bros. cigarette cards

Old golf buttons. These form an
attractive addition to golf
memorabilia. They are of many
metals: gold, silver-gilt, silver, bronze,
silver plate. Only members were
permitted to wear the Club button on
a blazer

Morrissian Ware vase — Height 8¾
inches Doulton

Pale green vase with tinted print by C. Dana Gibson (1867-1944) the American artist who immortalised the 'Gibson Girls' of English music-hall fame. The sketch is entitled 'Is a Caddie really necessary?' Made at Royal Doulton, England

Two dishes, with transfer prints of golfers. Made by Minton, England 1901

Punch bowl from Royal Blackheath
Golf Club (nineteenth-century) and
(below) enlargement of the escutcheon

Tea-caddy in Continental porcelain.
The decoration consists of part of 'The
Blackheath Golfer', a portrait of
William Innes and his caddie by
Lemuel Francis Abbott (1760-1803)

Two of the many coloured cartoons to illustrate The Rules of Golf, which were commissioned by the makers of Perrier Water: prints of them were used for advertising purposes. Perrier is a French company; on some of these cartoons the Rules are in both French and English

RULE XXXIII
A player ſhall not aſk for advice from anyone but his··caddie··nor ſhall he willingly be otherwiſe adviſed *in any way whatever*, ·
· · · · · · · · · ·
Copyright of "Perrier" Water

RULE·IV·
If a player play when his partner should have done so····
· · · · · · · · · ·
Copyright of "Perrier" Water

Then A Soldier. Full Of Strange Oaths ...

Seeking The Bubble Reputation Even In The Bunker's Mouth.

Then The Schoolboy With His Satchel And Shining Morning Face.

Two lithographs from a set entitled
'The Seven Ages of the Golfer'
produced by John Hassall (1868-1948).
A 'send-up' of Shakespeare

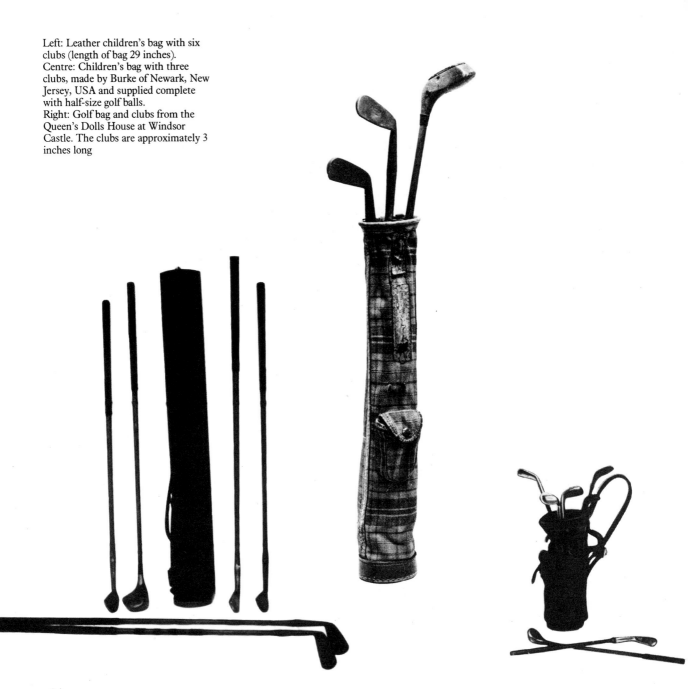

Left: Leather children's bag with six clubs (length of bag 29 inches).
Centre: Children's bag with three clubs, made by Burke of Newark, New Jersey, USA and supplied complete with half-size golf balls.
Right: Golf bag and clubs from the Queen's Dolls House at Windsor Castle. The clubs are approximately 3 inches long

Left: The wooden clubs from the golf bag in The Queen's Dolls House supported by the hand of the maker, Charles Gibson of Westward Ho!
Right: Three miniature golf clubs made by W.H. Way, one of Charles Gibson's apprentices, who subsequently emigrated to the USA and, in later life, became President of the U.S.P.G.A.

William M. Goddard – a figure from
Charles Lees' 'The Golfers: A Grand
Match Played Over St Andrews Links'